To

_____

From

_____

Date

_____

From the Becoming Anchored series

Tidings of Comfort and Joy

30 Devotionals for Christmas

Thomas Bratton

Butterfly Books Publishing

Tidings of Comfort and Joy: 30 Devotionals for Christmas
Copyright © Thomas Bratton 2024

Published by Butterfly Books Publishing. Butterfly Books Publishing is an independent publisher.

Cover Design by Butterfly Books Publishing
Interior Design by Butterfly Books Publishing
Edited and proofread by Butterfly Books Publishing
Photo Credits: Thomas Bratton

Printed in the United States of America

ISBN-13 (hardcover): 978-1-965652-00-8

All rights reserved. This publication is licensed for your personal enjoyment only. No part of this publication may be resold, reproduced, distributed, or transmitted in any form or by any means including photocopying, recording, or other electronic or mechanical methods without the prior written permission of the author, except in the case of brief quotations embodied in reviews or certain other non-commercial uses permitted by copyright law.

All scripture quotations, unless otherwise indicated, are taken from the New King James Version®. Copyright © 1982 by Thomas Nelson. Used by permission. All rights reserved.

Scripture quotations marked (NKJV) are taken from the Holy Bible, New International Version® NIV®. Copyright ©1973, 1978, 1984, 2011 by Biblica, Inc.™ Used by permission of Zondervan. All rights reserved worldwide. www.zondervan.com The "NIV" and "New International Version" are trademarks registered in the United States Patent and Trademark Office by Biblica, Inc.™

Scripture quotations marked (ERV) are taken from the HOLY BIBLE: EASY-TO-READ VERSION © 2001 by World Bible Translation Center, Inc. and used by permission.

Scripture quotations marked (NLT) are taken from the Holy Bible, New Living Translation, copyright ©1996, 2004, 2015 by Tyndale House Foundation. Used by permission of Tyndale House Publishers, Inc., Carol Stream, Illinois 60188. All rights reserved.

Scripture quotations marked (TLV) are taken from the Holy Scriptures, Tree of Life Version*. Copyright © 2014,2016 by the Tree of Life Bible Society. Used by permission of the Tree of Life Bible Society.

Scripture quotations taken from the New American Standard Bible® (NASB), Copyright © 1960, 1962, 1963, 1968, 1971, 1972, 1973, 1975, 1977, 1995 by The Lockman Foundation. Used by permission. Www.Lockman.org.

Contents

Foreword 1
Day 1 3
Day 2 5
Day 3 6
Day 4 7
Day 5 9
Day 6 11
Day 7 13
Day 8 15
Day 9 17
Day 10 19
Day 11 21
Day 12 23
Day 13 25
Day 14 26
Day 15 27
Day 16 29
Day 17 31
Day 18 33
Day 19 34
Day 20 35
Day 21 37
Day 22 39
Day 23 41
Day 24 43
Day 25 45
Day 26 47

Day 27	49
Day 28	51
Day 29	53
Day 30	55
Bonus	57
My Motivation to Write *Tidings of Comfort and Joy*	59
The Christmas Story Taken and Combined from the Gospels of Matthew and Luke	61
Guests	65
Gifts and Giving	66
Christmas Memories	67
Acts of Kindness	68
Additional Resources	69
Becoming Anchored	70
Thank You	71

Foreword

Christmas can be a mixed time of year. For some, it's a time of family, warmth, and celebration of different kinds. For others, it brings difficult challenges and increased stress. For others, it may even bring sadness and greater awareness of loved ones lost.

When Tom shared with me his heart for this devotional as a focus on the special memories and blessings of Christmas as a message of hope, I knew it would be something unique and special.

My prayer is that God will use it to touch your heart and remind you that you are never alone and that you are loved beyond anything you can imagine.

This devotional is full of special insights, encouragements, and reminders that no matter how Christmas looks for you, there is always joy and peace to be experienced by focusing on the true gift of Jesus. Everything else becomes an outpouring of His love and kind of a special bonus blessing.

Take each day in and remember His hope that lives within you through the mountains and the valleys.

Katelyn Silva – We Write Books
Author. Speaker. Mentor.

Day 1

All right then, the Lord himself will give you the sign. Look! The virgin will conceive a child! She will give birth to a son and will call him Immanuel (which means 'God is with us'). Isaiah 7:14 (NLT)

Isaiah's prophecies came to life just at the right time.

God is with us. Yes, indeed He is! Isaiah knew steadfast faith. God revealed Himself to him. He has before and still does today. However, how many people have the same faith as Isaiah did? Why the uncertainty? The only explanation I have is that we don't really listen. Sure, we go to church, listen to the sermon, maybe read a few Bible verses throughout the week, and try to live in a way God approves of. At least this is what we think. Am I right? Maybe we imagine what God might say if we were truly present to hear Him. Is the lack of being truly present because we might not like what He has to say?

We're instructed to fear the Lord: with love and respect. It's not fearing He will harm us, rather it's having such love and respect that we long to please Him and be in His presence. God loves us and wants the best for us. Usually better than we can imagine. In His time!

I listened to Joel Osteen the other day, and he said something that really got me thinking. Years ago, Joel went through something that was unfair, unjust, and left him wondering, '*Why me?*' I'm sure you can relate: "Why me?" right?! Well, 16 years later he encountered another situation; yes, 16 years. This time Joel went to battle prepared, not anxious for anything, and succeeded. This was the time Lakewood purchased the Compaq Center. He knows now that the incident he went through 16 years ago was to prepare him for when it mattered.

Are you prepared for when the Lord gives you a sign?

This Christmas season I encourage you – invite you – to spend some time with God.

THANK HIM. Thank God for His love, for His guidance, for protecting you and comforting you, and for the people He has placed in your life. Thank Him for everything He has blessed you with. Just thank Him.

Many people endure life as one catastrophe after another. If you're one of them, stop that negative thinking right now! Be excited for what God has planned for you. "'For I know the thoughts that I think toward you,' says the Lord, 'thoughts of peace and not of evil, to give you a future and a hope'" (Jeremiah 29:11).

Look for opportunities to help others with the gifts bestowed upon you. Your cup overflows!

Prayer

Lord, thank you for time to rest, time to revitalize my energy, time to get to know you more. A time to be with my family and friends. I pray for you to transform me into a new person by changing the way I think. Show me how to have more time for what is truly important in this life and the next, in Jesus', name Amen.

Day 2

The Christmas season is a time of thanksgiving, anticipation, and a time to reflect upon the relationships we have with others and with Jesus. The season begins with Advent – the expecting of the Messiah. We spend so much time staying busy with life; we're literally living in the fast lane. Our to-do lists are never-ending and it becomes overwhelming and literally controlling what we do and when.

There must be a time to stop! A time to be kind to others and to be kind to ourselves.

God wanted us to rest. God also wants us to bless others as He too has blessed you. God wants to be a part of your life in every aspect. Won't you invite Him into your life today?

Do your relationships with others reflect the goodness of Jesus?

How will you take time to refresh and rejuvenate so you can gain control of your life again? Will it include God?

Take inventory of the relationships you have. And ask yourself, who you see Jesus in, and do others see Jesus in you!

What relationships need nurturing?

For even the Son of Man came not to be served but to serve others and to give his life as a ransom for many. Mark 10:45

Prayer

Lord, thank you for time to rest, time to revitalize my energy, time to get to know you more. A time to be with my family and friends. I pray for you to transform me into a new person by changing the way I think. Show me how to have more time for what is truly important in this life and the next, in Jesus', name, Amen.

Day 3

Mary had great faith and found favor with God. Despite being a virgin and about to be married to Joseph, a descendant of King David, how would she explain the pregnancy? Mary trusted God that everything would work according to His plans. Mary went to Joseph and told him, "An angel appeared and said I will give birth to a son, and we will call him Jesus."

Joseph was contemplating whether he should marry Mary. And then an angel appeared to him and told him not to fear and that Mary was the one chosen. The angel told Joseph to go ahead with the marriage.

Joseph's obedience also took great faith.

"Now faith is the substance of things we hoped for, the evidence of things not seen." Hebrews 11:1

Remember this:

God has a plan for us too. Even through a time of adversity when things seem to be difficult to comprehend, stay in faith as Mary did. And with confidence, we will achieve great things according to God's will for us, by living righteously and having faith.

Prayer

Father, we thank you for your promises and unfailing love for us. Please give us the kind of faith Mary had and help us learn to trust you more, even through difficult times. In Jesus' name, amen.

Day 4

Have you read the story of Jesus this holiday season? Worship Him throughout the day through scripture and prayer, meditation, and journaling your thoughts. **Jesus** is the **reason** for the **season.**

Ask Jesus, "Where is my place here on earth? How can I become a better servant to you Lord?" Take time to sit quietly and journal what He says to your spirit.

All too often we get involved in all the commotion during the Christmas season. Preparing for family gatherings; seeing friends, new and old, and all the gifts we believe are a necessity to give to others; shopping and preparing meals; and we also want to look our best when we gather with others, when we are entertaining, or when going to an event. The list goes on and on and on.

We work and have families who depend on us for many things. We remember loved ones lost and grieve. We try to be kind to others and make a good impression on the ones who treat us poorly. We meet with people we are not fond of, yet we put on that smile and play the part.

Hmm. Just thinking about trying to make everything perfect is stressful and we miss the significance of what is truly important. We know there's a problem only when we are so stressed; we're grumpy, tired, and short-tempered.

Back in the days when Jesus was ministering to others, a woman named Martha invited Jesus into her home and was very busy preparing a wonderful meal for Him. Mary, Martha's sister, was sitting next to Jesus listening and making Him a priority by spending time with Him. Martha became jealous and angry that Mary was spending time with Jesus instead of helping her – because she wanted time with Jesus too! Luke 10:38-42.

How do we handle and manage our time to be in the company of our guests, people we want to spend time with, yet take care of them hospitably also?

Frist, separate "handle" and "manage". Manage with how to take your ideas from preparation to execution. Begin with a list and leave the rest to God. He will let you know what is truly important so you can handle your expectations and emotions better, so you won't be disappointed. Remember the "**Reason** for the **Season**"

When was the last time you spent time alone with Jesus?

Prayer

Jesus, we are in awe of you, our "Messiah". I ask that during all the busyness of the Christmas season, help me not to get lost in all the preparation and planning. Don't allow it to deny me the privilege to be with you. Let me exemplify your love so others may open their hearts to you. Let this be a time we celebrate you and not be hurried, or anxious about anything. Let this be a time we put aside everything that does not reflect your goodness, kindness and love. In Jesus' name, Amen.

Day 5

God is Love, Love is Kind

Have you heard Christmas is a magical time of the year? We have so much to be grateful for, and Christmas is a time of joy - bringing peace to us all. God is a loving God – the Bible says, "God is love (1 John 4:8) and that love is kind (1 Cor. 13:4). Whatever you are going through, He promises to bring you peace. He wants us to be at peace and not anxious for anything. What more could you hope for with the amazing gifts God has already blessed you with?

One of the blessings of Christmas is to gather with friends and family. It's time to give thanks. There is so much magic in the air at Christmas. Partaking in the freshly baked pies and cookies at, children unwrapping Santa's gifts, a quiet Christmas Eve watching it snow. These are just a few of the things we hope for when we put all our hope into Jesus.

Do you have a personal relationship with Jesus?
How do you express your love to others?
When was the last time you baked something for your neighbor?

*"And you must **love** the LORD your God with all your heart, all your soul, all your mind, and all your strength. The second is equally important: **'Love** your neighbor as yourself.' No other commandment is greater than these." (Mark 12:30-31 NIV).*

Take time this holiday season to do something nice for someone else, even if you don't feel like it. Remember that Jesus came into this world to serve others; we should follow his example.

Prayer

Heavenly Father, thank you for all you have done for me and my family. Thank you for such wonderful neighbors. Thank you for my friend's. I pray you will bless them and let them know how much they are loved by you. And when the Christmas season unfolds and comes to a close, may you bless us all with your love and give us the opportunities to share that love every day of the year. In Jesus name, Amen.

Day 6

Expectancy is something we all look forward to. Joeseph and Mary looked forward to being blessed with the birth of the Messiah. Little baby Jesus was the Messiah the prophets foretold would come into the world as a little baby, would be our teacher, would free us from this sinful world and would be our savior. The wise men also heard of the coming of Jesus and were working late one evening when they heard a voice and looked up to the sky, finding the star that led them to where Jesus was with His parents.

Having a baby is a time of celebration and a blessing to the family. I remember my mom would marvel at babies; they brought her such joy. They say nothing beings greater joy than a newborn baby. I can still see the way her face would light up as she played with one of her grandbabies. There is really nothing more adorable than a baby's smile at you.

My brother recently became a grandfather earlier this year. There is nothing grander than becoming a grandparent for the first time. It's like reliving the past as you recall having your own children. Small bundles of joy to have fun playing with while you watch them grow and learn new things. Along the way babies are so funny, you can't help but just laugh with them and cuddle them. My brother tells me how this little granddaughter is like a breath of fresh air. He is forever grateful to have raised his own children and now to have a granddaughter. He would do anything for her and nothing is more important to him than his family.

How do a baby's expressions make you feel?
Just like the expectations of Jesus, don't you feel the same anticipation when you or someone you know is having a baby?

For unto us a Child is born,
Unto us a Son is given;
And the government will be upon His shoulder.
And His name will be called
Wonderful, Counselor, Mighty God,
Everlasting Father, Prince of Peace.
    Isaiah 9:6

Prayer

Heavenly Father, thank you for the joy of babies, the feelings we have during the mother's expectancy, bringing hope, as we expect the miraculous gift of a newborn. As we celebrate Christmas this year let us remember the anticipation of those awaiting the birth of Jesus and the hope, He brought to the world then and now, in Jesus' name, Amen.

Day 7

God is pleased with you when you show kindness to others. Be patient, compassionate with others and do not think of yourself as better than them but show genuine concern for others – not just throughout the holiday season. Be this person every day, so others will see God through you.

You can exemplify who God is by letting someone go before you in line, opening the door for someone, lending a helping hand to your neighbor, or by listening and being there for someone in need. How have you felt when there was no one to listen to you during a difficult time? Lonely? But when God places someone in your life that loneliness evaporates and instead you feel seen, heard, and loved.

When your kind to others, they will be kind to you. Life is a reflection of yourself. Reflect the Love that God has for you so that His light may shine through you.

Remember the sayings: "what goes around comes around" and "Do not unto others as you do not want others to do unto you"?

This Christmas season allow God's light to shine upon you so you may be a blessing to others. It is often considered acceptable to just be the receiver of blessings. However, do not let your giving be for a particular reason, even if that reason is the blessings that come! Give generously for the sake of giving and joy. God knows your heart and you know yourself of any selfish desires you have. Let go of these selfish desires and pray.

Please accept the gift of giving to be your blessing.

*"And I know it is important to **love** him with all my heart and all my understanding and all my strength, and to **love** my neighbor as myself. This is more important than to offer all the burnt offerings and sacrifices required in the law." Mark 12:33. (NLT)*

Prayer

Heavenly Father, thank you so very much for your understanding, your compassion and love for me and others. I pray with your help I too will be a person that shows kindness to others. Search my heart O' Lord and know it's true and help me clean my garden of any selfish desires. In Jesus name, Amen.

Day 8

The night before Christmas can be exhausting and yet exhilarating making last-minute preparations for the following day. Rather than thinking of carving the turkey, devote a little time to doing something that will bring some peace and tranquility to reduce the stress. Remember the reason for the season. If you're stressed then, it probably isn't pleasing to the Lord either. Ask for His guidance and thank Him for all He has done.

Stress may come from being overwhelmed, especially during the holidays. It's nice for our family and friends so they may enjoy the festivities too. However, we need to remind ourselves that we deserve the same pleasures with them.

What are some ways to ensure you have a VERY Merry Christmas with the ones you love?

Go ahead and make a list of what you enjoy. Contemplate the idea of getting some help from your guests – your family – so everyone is pitching in. And you know what? When other people are included, they feel more appreciated. Entrust them with helping with dinner, cleaning up afterwards, or maybe helping with the decorations. Why don't you give it a try?

Make this a Christmas to be memorable for years to come.

"Don't worry about anything; instead, pray for everything. Tell God what you need and thank him for all he has done. Then you will experience God's peace, which exceeds anything we can understand. His peace will guard your hearts and minds as you live in Christ Jesus." Philippian's 4:6-7. (NLT)

Prayer

Lord, thank you for each and every day. Help me to remember and be present at Christmas. Help me to have the right balance of being a good host and also enjoying all the good things you have given for Christmas. In Jesus name, Amen.

Day 9

I met a friend at church who is a local to the small community and a family man. He lives just outside of town and works his own land. Not too many wholesome people nowadays work on their own land. Our church has a Stephen Ministry program where I first met him, and I was the care receiver. It was nice to meet with him and we soon became friends, while he showed me around the church and met many people. I also became a Stephen Minister myself.

Years later he was talking, when he suddenly proposed to his lovely girlfriend at the time. She is now his wife and companion of thirty years. The proposal was after six years and was on Christmas day before consummating the marriage.

On that day, my friend and his soon-to-be fiancé were opening gifts Christmas morning when suddenly, someone said, "There is another package in the tree!" All eyes were eagerly waiting for her to open the gift. As she did, a bear sitting on a block of ice with a fishing pole was revealed. Everyone was saying, "Look, look, there's something tied to the end."

Right then, my friend got down on his knees and proposed with the question, "Would you marry me?"

She said, "Yes, yes, I will I love you with all my heart."

With tears flowing during this emotional surprise, he realized then how blessed he was. To this day, he remarks how marrying her has changed his life.

Have you been surprised at Christmas, or surprised someone else with a gift?

What blessings do you hold close to your heart at Christmas that changed your life?

The man who finds a wife finds a treasure, and he receives favor from the LORD. Proverbs 18:22 (NLT)

Prayer

Heavenly Father, Christmas is a supernatural time of the year. Let this Christmas be no different. Let your peace spread your loving kindness through the world this day and every day after. Lord, we need a little joy in our lives. So many disasters have occurred, sadness, loneliness, and homelessness. Please, please Lord, Let the star that led the wisemen to Jesus' shine brightly this Christmas season bringing hope, peace, and joy to all. In Jesus' name, Amen.

Day 10

Throughout the year we have celebrated many victories and accomplishments and have received joy along the way, but we may have made some mistakes too. I invite and encourage you to forget these, and to instead focus on and be thankful for all that God has done and wear the blessings He has poured out upon you well.

Sometimes the most important thing we forget is to be grateful for our health. A dear friend of mine had Bell's palsy, a neurological disorder that causes paralysis of one side of the face. This lasted for a few months. She would still go to work and endure the pain and discomfort that came with paralysis. One of her children happened to be graduating from boot camp at the time and she didn't hesitate to board a plane so she could be there with her daughter. She continued to make the best of each situation and with prayers, she rose above this neurological disorder and is grateful to God for helping her along the way. This reminds me of the poem "Footprints in the Sand". When you only see one set of prints in the sand, that is when Jesus carried you! Rise above the illness.

We all have struggles throughout life and yet we're all on a different journey. Some struggles are not as bad as others, while some may be totally irreversible and difficult to move forward. We know with God all things are possible and so we put our trust and faith in Him.

How do you overcome some of life's struggles?
What do you need to let go of to move forward with His grace?
Have you thanked God for helping you?

"I have not achieved it, but I focus on this one thing: Forgetting the past and looking forward to what lies ahead, I press on to reach the end of the race and receive the heavenly prize for which God, through Christ Jesus, is calling us." Philippians 3:13-14.

Prayer

Heavenly Father, thank you for all you have done for me and all you have planned for me this coming year. Help me to let go of my past hurts and mistakes with an open heart to receive your blessing. Strengthen me through the challenges and grant me a heart of gratitude that I would not take anything for granted. Let me to be a blessing upon others and to give glory to you, in Jesus' name, Amen.

Day 11

But Jesus told him, "No! The Scriptures say, 'People do not live by bread alone, but by every word that comes from the mouth of God.'"
Mathew 4:4 (NLT)

Jesus invites us to live according to the word of God. And He lived this out as our perfect example. During the Christmas season is often a time to demonstrate this to others in the way we behave – maybe while out shopping or for those who are suffering during this time of year. But sometimes, it's not always easy or obvious to know what it looks like to "live according to the Word of God."

To begin with, Love God with all your heart, soul, mind, and strength. Follow Him and the example of Christ, like that old saying "what would Jesus do?" Love others as He loves you: unconditionally. See others through His eyes. Do not judge! Be kind, be merciful, and be humble.

Ask the Holy Spirit to help you live according to the fruits of the spirit (Galatians 5:22-23). Believe it! Receive it by faith. And when you find yourself having a difficult time to live according to the Spirit and the word of God, pray without ceasing!

Afterall, while the Christmas season is an excellent time to be reminded of these truths, it isn't the only time to live this way. We are called to live it out every day of the year!

In what way do you find it difficult to live a life of obedience?
Humble yourselves and ask for forgiveness. Be the person others want to be.
Do others see God through you?
In what ways has living by God's word been fruitful in your life?

Prayer

Heavenly Father, I don't need to tell you how difficult it is at times to live by your word in today's world. For that I am sorry and ask for your forgiveness. Please remind me when I am having a difficult time that you are the only one who can bring me clarity. I pray I will see others through your eyes and be there for them as you are for me. In Jesus' name, Amen.

Day 12

Christmas isn't just one day. Many know this – after all, after Thanksgiving is often called the "Christmas Season"! There are so many activities, music is playing of a different tune everywhere, and the anticipation builds like nothing else!

But the actual celebration often culminates in that one special day – whatever it might look like for different people in different parts of the world.

For one of my friends and her family, they celebrate Christmas two or three times over the holidays!

She shared with me that many years ago, her oldest son was born on Christmas day, her own beautiful, blessed gift from God. She wanted to make him feel like it was just as special on Christmas as if he had been born some other day. She experienced God's care and providence in even the small things as her prayer was answered.

Each year for Christmas, they celebrate in El Paso with Mexican traditions, one of which is that Christmas is celebrated on Christmas Eve. So, when they visit family for Christmas, they celebrate on Christmas Eve with the family and all its flurry of activities, socialization, and fun, presents from relatives included!

Then, on Christmas Day, they spend some time together in the morning for Christmas and afterward, the day is a birthday celebration. They even give separate presents to her son designated just for his birthday.

Because there is so much activity with family during their trip, she and her husband reserve their presents for their children for their own day together once they return home. They then often spend a day together where they read the Christmas story – the true and greatest gift and meaning of Christmas in our Lord and Savior Jesus – and have their own food and gifts to celebrate.

Whether it's more elaborate or simple, they take time to remember the greatest blessings in life and the things that really matter in the view of eternity. Ultimately, we are not just members of an earthly family, but members of the eternal family of God!

Whatever your Christmas does include, take time to reflect on the gift of Christ Jesus in whom we have all spiritual blessings and are seated in Heavenly places and through whom we can say to the King of the universe, "Abba, Father!" with boldness and confidence.

Do you have a birthday on Christmas or know someone who does? How do you make it special?

What is something special you and your family do for Christmas?

Prayer

Heavenly Father, thank you that I can come into your throne room with boldness and make my requests known to you through Jesus. Help me to remember the greatest gift and to honor you in all the celebration with family and friends. Thank you for the gift of loved ones we get to enjoy life with. Help me point them toward you and give you glory. In Jesus' name, Amen.

Day 13

Love! God loves us so much He sacrificed His son for us so we may be saved and have a relationship with Him through Jesus. So that we may tell others about what He has done for us. This is the whole reason He came as a baby.

Most of us, however, are quick to judge others and gossip about them. Instead, remembering what Christ did for us, we should share the love of Jesus to everyone, even when someone is different than us. Let us keep that in mind when we gather with others at Christmas.

Let's not forget we are all on a different path. We all have trials and experiences to learn from. Being kind doesn't cost anything, but being there for someone is the greatest gift you can give.

Who do you know that you have looked at unfairly and judged them?
What is love?
In what ways can you show love to everyone, without judgement?

God sent his Son into the world not to judge the world, but to save the world through him. John 3:17 (NLT)

Prayer

Heavenly Father, I am grateful for you and your son Jesus. I pray I would be more like Him and show the kindness that is from you and your Son. I pray I would not be a gossiper and that I would step away when anyone judges others. Help me learn not to participate in judging others or gossip. Help me instead to spread the word of God and your love, in Jesus' name, Amen.

Day 14

In the sixth month of Elizabeth's pregnancy, God sent the angel Gabriel to Nazareth, a town in Galilee, to a virgin pledged to be married to a man named Joseph, a descendant of David. The virgin's name was Mary. The angel went to her and said, "Greetings, you who are highly favored! The Lord is with you." Luke 1:26-28 (NIV)

God's divine grace came just at the right time - a time of turmoil, evil, violence, and people turning their backs to God, which had been foretold by the prophets, hundreds of years ago.

God's ways are higher than ours.
Before the coming of the Messiah, people would make sacrifices for their sins yet would continue to sin.
Jesus came at just the right time, making the ultimate sacrifice to save people then, now, and always.
At that time, Mary had a visit from Gabriel, informing her she would give birth to the Messiah, "Jesus."
Now we know God uses others to intervene, help, and speak to us.
God also uses ordinary people to do amazing things.

What amazing things has God blessed you with?
Who has God used to speak to you? Has God used you to do something amazing for someone you know?
Take time to reflect today and be open to the Lord blessing you so you may be a blessing to others.

Prayer

Father in Heaven, thank you for Christ and for the forgiveness of sins. Let me remember the day when Jesus was born into this sinful world to show us how to live. Please keep the evil one from us and prompt us to make the choices that bring honor to you. In Jesus' name, Amen.

Day 15

For some, Christmas isn't the same as it was. Let's face it: we're too busy trying to impress others with gifts, Christmas gatherings and parties and event plannings. We spend less time than ever remembering what Christmas is all about: The Lord, our Savior! Gathering with friends and family to celebrate doesn't need to always include gifts and such. God wanted us to gather and celebrate by being there for others, supporting each other and just spending time together.

A friend of mine told me she struggles at Christmas. Being divorced, one child is estranged and the other makes rare appearances. With not much other family, she relies upon a few friends to get her through. It doesn't replace the large family gatherings she once enjoyed. Unfortunately, this is becoming more common. It is difficult because we don't want to impose on others, but we desperately need each other during the Holidays. We need others all year long.

Preparing for Christmas can be stressful Thankfully we have Jesus to celebrate the journey with us.

Do you know someone who is alone at Christmas?
How can you make a difference to someone who struggles during the Christmas season?
What brings you joy at Christmas?

And a voice from heaven said, "This is my dearly loved Son, who brings me great joy." Matthew 3:17. (NLT)

John the Baptist prepared the way for Jesus, and now Jesus prepares a home for us through Him to the Father. What joy we have in knowing we can find salvation through our faith in Jesus Christ our Savior.

Prayer

Dear God, help me not to struggle with the feeling of sadness through the holidays. Especially when I notice other families gathering together having a joyous time and celebrating the birth of Jesus. Help me to focus on you and the joy that you have already given, In Jesus' name, Amen.

Day 16

Sometimes God's plan may not make sense to you at the time. Do not hurry to take matters into your own hands. Wow! I've made this mistake before. Many times.

We can be so impatient when making a decision. Often the biggest decisions of our life are the ones we hastily go ahead with an idea, change of career, retirement savings, even medical ones. We tend to allow others to persuade us to move forward immediately and other times we just talk ourselves right into it.

Imagine if you were suffering from addiction and wanted help not to pick up that drink again. So, there is the 12-step program many follow and some relapse. Others don't bother at all and think they can do it on their own. If only we put God first. He knows you're suffering and wants to help you if you let Him.

My wife is a recovering alcoholic and celebrating her 20th year anniversary and is so grateful God has given her another chance. She has memories of when things were not so good. The biggest consequences were losing her first marriage, losing custody of her adorable children and being imprisoned. The rule is "one day at a time". She now has a wonderful life and helps others struggling with the same addictions and similar consequences.

Patience is a virtue when making a decision and we all know when we put God first His plans will always work to the good when you trust Him and stay in faith.

During the Holidays is a wonderful time to reflect and give thanks to God for all He has done and continues to do. If you're struggling financially and want to purchase gifts, God will find a way. If you're having guests over but don't have a lot of time to put it all together, God will find a way. If you lost your job, someone you love is in the hospital, or you want to volunteer to help others but have little time, God will find a way, just as He has for others going through what you are going through.

Have you ever wondered why He puts people in someone's life? He uses people who have gone through similar situations so when God blesses you, use that blessing to be a blessing to help someone who needs the same help you once did.

Who can you help this Christmas?
What has God helped you through?

The mind of a man plans his way, but the Lord shows him what to do. Proverbs 16:9 (NLV)

Prayer

Father God, I will be forever grateful for what you have done for me, your wisdom bestowed upon me, your loving kindness to pick me up again and again. Help me be a blessing to others as you have blessed me. Christmas is so difficult for so many people. Please look after them and if it is your will, guide me so I may help them too, in Jesus' name, Amen.

Day 17

As joyous as the birth of Jesus is, it's also a sobering reminder of Jesus' ultimate sacrifice of His life for ours. While many of us wouldn't sacrifice our own lives for someone, especially a stranger, we may sacrifice our life for someone we know and hold close to our heart.

First responders, the military and public servants risk their lives every day to protect us. Many of them sacrifice greatly during the holiday season in order to serve when they could otherwise spend time with their own loved ones.

There are similar sacrifices we make for our families. We get in the car and put us in harm's way going to the grocer for food to feed our families. We go to work to provide a means of support to pay for the groceries, the home we live in, and even the automobile we drive to and from places.

There are other sacrifices we make too. Many are smaller, sometimes not even noticeable ones. I imagine you can think of some sacrifices others have made to be of service.

Let's remember to be kind and grateful for those who sacrifice in our lives and communities and do something to be a blessing to them also.

What sacrifices have you made?
Who can you be of service to?

"Take your son, your only son—yes, Isaac, whom you **love** *so much—and go to the land of Moriah. Go and sacrifice him as a burnt offering on one of the mountains, which I will show you." Genesis 22:2*

Prayer

Heavenly Father, thank you for sacrificing Jesus so we can be cleansed and free from our sins. I also pray for the people whose job it is to help others and protect us by risking their lives. Bless them dear Lord, and let their good deeds not go unnoticed. Help me find ways to make sacrifices to be a blessing to others even if it is a small sacrifice or if it goes unnoticed, I pray in Jesus' name, Amen.

Day 18

As I sit on my front porch at night, I marvel at the stars, wondering what the wise men were thinking. They knew it was time for baby Jesus to be born. So, they left for their search to find the Messiah. How exciting this was during that time! God's plans never fail or elude us. He reveals all He does beforehand to His friends.

Sometimes when I'm looking out at the stars, I wish I had the same clarity as the wise men did. But it is only when we are expecting God's best for us that we experience everything we have hoped for and more.

Only when we have trust in the Lord will He take delight in our dreams. Faith please Him! (Hebrews 11:6).

This Christmas I invite you to sit and watch the stars or find a place of solitude and imagine anything is possible with God.

What experiences have you discovered pondering upon the stars?

I encourage you to journal your thoughts and soon you'll see blessings after blessings follow.

What are your hopes, dreams, and aspirations?

Trust in the LORD with all your heart; do not depend on your own understanding. Proverbs 3:5.

Prayer

Heavenly Father, I look back and wonder what must have transpired when Jesus was born an infant and people traveled afar to see with their own eyes. How I marvel at the awesomeness of everything you do, please help me to always tell your story to others in a way that is pleasing to you, even when I am tired after all the worldly traditions of Christmas have ended, let your story continue, in Jesus' name, Amen...

Day 19

When I was younger, I didn't give much thought to anything other than what I wanted for myself. This was very shallow thinking and dangerous. Living a God-centered life is the only way to have a more meaningful and rewarding life. I really didn't know what living to serve others was all about, until being introduced to fellow believers and becoming involved with opportunities to serve at Church and being fed the word of God through Bible study.

Living for God is being obedient to His ways. Love God, love others! They say joy comes in the morning. Living to be of service to others brings joy to everyone, including yourself and God. Serving others is pleasing to God. Serving others is necessary to show your loving kindness to the world.

Look for opportunities in your local community and in this season to volunteer or be of service.

In what ways can you be of service to someone this week? This Christmas season?
Have you begun a Bible study recently? If not, when?

As I learn your righteous regulations, I will thank you by living as I should! Psalm 119:7 (NLT)

Prayer

Heavenly Father, what a joy it is to share your love with others through serving them whenever the opportunity comes my way. Thank you and please continue to give me these opportunities to help someone today and always, in Jesus' name, Amen.

Day 20

Romans 12 begins by instructing us to be a living sacrifice. I love how the Apostle Paul's letter to the Romans is an example of the sermon on the mount with Jesus teaching us about values and how to live. Jesus wanted us to live with hope and expectancy of greater things to come. But we must do our part too. We must live accordingly to His words, His teachings, and with love for God and others, which is summed up in the law of the prophets.

It is my aspiration to live in accord to that of Jesus, To take delight in the Lord, honor Him, respect Him and live in a Christ-like manner that others would notice Christ living through me. I hope you share the same values as I do and love God and love others as yourself.

Christmas always seems to be a time when people are a little friendlier, more forgiving, more kind as the Holidays embark upon us. Won't you join me and the many other Christians and spread the good news of Jesus?

Enjoy time to reflect upon your life and the life Jesus wants for you. Read some scripture and journal your thoughts that come to your heart. Bring joy to others, help them, spend time with people. Get to know their story. You'll see they're not much different than you!

What does a living sacrifice mean to you?
How can you express your love for others in a way that you will reflect the love of Jesus?

Be devoted to one another in love. Honor one another above yourselves. Romans 12:10

Prayer

Heavenly Father, this Christmas let us remember the true meaning of Christmas. A time to rejoice in the Lord and to express our love for Him. A time to be an example of Christ's love unto others we encounter through this season and every day of the year, in Jesus' name, Amen.

Day 21

Because of Jesus, we have the opportunity to experience intimacy with God through the Holy Spirit. The veil was torn!

When you're reading scripture, praying, or meditating on God's Word, there is a sense of peace that transcends through your spirit. You are filled with joy which only comes from the Holy Spirit. The most gratifying feeling is when others see Jesus through you when they are in your presence. There is a calmness which has no other explanation than that your spirit is filled with the fruit of the Holy Spirit.

A friend of mine begins her day with some friends in a bible study group. She has never experienced the radiance of the Lord's Spirit within her as much as she does now. My friend has always been a confident and strong woman, sociable and well respected. Now she is forever filled with thanksgiving, living a life of the fruit of the Spirit. Her team member, clients, friends and family have all witnessed this amazing transformation take place. It's no wonder when you really study God's word you feel the words come alive! This is what it is and much more when filled with the Spirit.

Living a life in accordance with the word of God is the greatest feeling, knowing He is waking with you always and forever.

I encourage you to pick up the Bible, open it up wherever it may be, and start reading what the scripture is saying to you. It does, always has, and always will be the living word of God.

This Christmas would be a great time to read to yourself, with others, with your children the Christmas story. The greatest story ever told.

May the God of hope fill you with all joy and peace as you trust in Him, so that you may overflow with hope by the power of the Holy Spirit. Romans 15:13 (NIV)

Prayer

Lord, I am forever blessed to be filled with the Spirit. Thank you for this gift. I am truly blessed to have come to know you in the most intimate ways. Thank you for being with me wherever I go, so if I stumble, I will not fall. I pray the gifts you have bestowed upon me would be seen by others so they will come to know you the way I do. Let this Christmas bring hope, joy, peace to everyone, so they too will feel your spirit so they may live a life according to your word. In Jesus' name, Amen.

Day 22

Have you ever heard someone say, "Thank God it's morning?" And some say, "Oh God it's morning." Now I'm not sure it is said quite like that, but you notice the difference. Attitude is the new gratitude. Positivity is an attitude. The Power of Positive Thinking by "Norman Vincent Peale Is one of the most powerful books I have ever read. Simply by keeping a positive mindset and having an intimate relationship with God, everything changes.

Let me tell you a story of another friend of mine.

So, this friend from Atlanta told me that before she goes anywhere or begins her day, she invites God to go with her everywhere she goes and to be with her in all she does. A few years back when I first met her, she was in sales and involved in groups, some political, and this was the foundation where she began to establish many relationships, ones she nourishes by helping them. Sometimes it may be by making a suggestion or buying them a coffee. She knows people's time is valuable. and she found a niche were putting others first will come back to you. Her commitment to help others took off fast. She has become a success rather quickly. It was through God and her commitment to others, her determination to serve others purposefully, that her success took off like wildfire.

Imagine what would have been if she tried to do this on her own. Her heart was in the right place already. But with God she flourished. But with God all things are possible. Matthew 19:26(TLV)

When I'm out and about I notice the hurriedness of the world. Except at Christmas time. Everyone seems a bit friendlier then, calmer, and more kind. Imagine a world we live in being like, well, like Christmas every day of the year.

If we viewed the world through God's eyes, what would you see?
When hosting a Christmas gathering, who do you try to impress?

Who do you take an interest in, not just at Christmas, but all through the year?

Then make me truly happy by agreeing wholeheartedly with each other, loving one another, and working together with one mind and purpose. Don't be selfish; don't try to impress others. Be humble, thinking of others as better than yourselves. Don't look out only for your own interests, but take an interest in others, too. Philippians 2:2-4 (NLT)

Prayer

Heavenly Father, help me to be humble and not think of myself as better than others. Help me to show an interest in others first, even when it is difficult. Help me to see everyone through your eyes, so they would see your compassion, your kindness and your love through me, Lord, every day of the year. I ask you to go with me everywhere, in Jesus' name, Amen...

Day 23

Christmas is a time of giving, a time with friends and families, a time to gather at work parties, a time to worship with our church families. Exchanging gifts, sharing meals, sharing memories, sharing a few laughs, gazing at children eagerly awaiting to open their gifts, is all part of the spirit of giving

Or is it! Let us remember that all of it is because of the true gift of Jesus - the reason for the season. Sure, all the gatherings, gifts and parties are fine, so long we're putting God first. Like any other time, we should put God first, right? Then let's be sure to celebrate the birth of Jesus.

At Christmas, my mentor from Atlanta and her family don't partake in exchanging gifts, meals or anything alike for themselves until they sing happy birthday to Jesus. Birthday cake and all. They include Him in all their activities. They put God first and celebrate the true meaning of Christmas. The reason for the season! When exchanging gifts amongst each other, they are not the typical gifts like a sweater, gadget for the kitchen or some other gift that may likely be returned. They buy gifts that make memories. Concert tickets, favorite restaurants, sporting and theatre gifts. These gifts may only be used once in many cases, but they are a gift one can experience. Will you remember who gave you that wrong sized sweater in a color you don't like, or will you remember the one you said, "Here, go have some fun with a friend."

What memories do you share with your family and friends?

Do you remember the Christmas story? Read the story of Christmas from the bible. I have included it here in this book as you journey through the greatest season here on earth.

On coming to the house, they saw the child with his mother Mary, and they bowed down and worshipped him. Then they opened their treasures and presented him with gifts of gold, frankincense and myrrh. Matthew 2:11 (NIV)

Prayer

Father in heaven, thank you for the birth of baby Jesus and the hope He brings to us for generations to come until eternity. Help us recognize Him this day as we celebrate along with our friends and families as we partake in this feast. We are thankful for your blessings which shine upon us each day. Even in the darkest of times you provide a lamp to our feet. Bless dear Lord with these thy gifts. Let us also remember those less fortunate than us, the lonely, the widowed, and the sick on this most Holy days we pray for Jesus and seek His kingdom forever and ever, in Jesus' name, Amen.

Day 24

Christmas is the most wonderful time of the year. Although, at times, it may not seem that way when we feel hurried, stressed and overwhelmed. Therefore, do not let our minds wander and think of all the things that bother us and the people we find annoying.

We have all heard "what comes around, goes around" will ultimately come back to you in the same manner. You notice everywhere you go: the grocer, that person at work, and especially the way people drive - which has led to road rage all too often – can easily stack up your sense of annoyance and stress? We have our own synchronicities as we plan family gatherings, meeting with friends you may have not seen for a long time, going to the store, buying gifts and the list goes on and on.

Rather than letting those small annoyances bring you down, I encourage you to reflect on all the positive memories of Christmas and on Christ Himself.

Christmas is to be centered around the Lord. After all it is His birthday. God's gift to us. His blessings are anew every morning. So be kind, patient and show empathy for those who are a bit stressed. You don't know what someone is going through.

Do you reflect the same love for others as God does for us?

Keep to a plan and follow accordingly allowing enough time to allow yourself time to enjoy the season with peace among yourself and others.

How will you let go of any animosity?

"Don't judge others, and God will not judge you. Don't condemn others, and you will not be condemned. Forgive others, and you will be forgiven. Give to others, and you will receive. You will be given much. It will be poured into your hands—more than you can hold. You will be

given so much that it will spill into your lap. The way you give to others is the way God will give to you." Luke 6:37-38 (ERV)

Prayer

Father in heaven, help me to remember the reason for which we celebrate Christmas above all else. To be forgiving as you forgive us. Not to judge or condemn! To treat everyone with the same kindness, compassion, and respect we would want ourselves in return, in Jesus' name, Amen.

Day 25

CHRISTMAS DAY

For years my wife and I lived in a small town outside of Ann Arbor, Michigan. We belonged to Dexter United Methodist Church. Christmas time was always my favorite time at Church. It's easy to forget about the meaning of Christmas, but not at Church. There are so many ways to help so many people and touch them in a way that keeps hope alive.

We engaged time volunteering with "Angel Tree". We would have upwards of 100 children with a parent who was incarcerated. With a mission, they helped children by providing a couple of gifts in the name of whichever parent may not be able to present a gift otherwise. Many of the congregation would purchase gifts for these children and wrap them for another person to deliver the gifts. The greatest gift of this mission was to deliver the gift(s) to the family and see their smiles light up like Christmas morning.

There was something for everyone to share their time to help others have a wonderful Christmas, such as filling shoe boxes for children across the world. We hosted for the entire community with Christmas dinners, a live nativity, and the list goes on.

Our Christmas services were also a favorite. Children played a big role too. The Worship band, those who rang bells, singing along to Christmas songs and of course, Silent Night.

What are your favorite memories of Church at Christmas time?
How can you bring joy to Christmas?
Do you volunteer at Church? In your community?

The angel reassured them. "Don't be afraid!" he said. "I bring you good news that will bring great joy to all people. The Savior—yes, the Messiah, the Lord—has been born today in Bethlehem, the city of David! And you will recognize him by this sign: You will find a baby wrapped snugly in strips of cloth, lying in a manger." Luke 2:10-12. (NLT)

Prayer

Heavenly Father, thank you for the gift of Jesus, the gift of life, and the gift of salvation so that I may be saved. Thank you that Jesus lives through me, opening the door to salvation, allowing me the opportunity to have an intimate relationship with you. I choose to be obedient to your ways, which are better than my own, and I am thankful for your many blessings, that I may share the same love you have for me with others, in Jesus' name, Amen.

Day 26

Santa Claus is a fictional character whose story brings children all over the world happiness at Christmas. And some adults too. After all, we need some happy moments too. But the expression on young children's faces and the glimmer in their eyes is priceless. They light up like a Christmas tree, as my nephew experienced when he was a toddler.

My brother, now deceased, and his wife used to lay down a sleeping bag for my nephew under the tree and let him gaze at the tree from underneath while he fell asleep, as if it was part of a fantasy or sleeping under the stars. While he fell asleep under the tree, they would watch and hope all his dreams were magical. They continued this tradition for a few years and always take delight in their son as if he was lying in a manager under the stars wrapped in cloth.

Where Santa Claus is fun, let us also remember that Jesus is real and alive today and continues to give of all the heavenly blessings to His children every day.

What memories do you remember growing up as a child?
Do you know the Christmas story?
What traditions do you have, or have you began any new traditions?

After the wise men heard the king, they left. They saw the same star they had seen in the east, and they followed it. The star went before them until it stopped above the place where the child was. They were very happy and excited to see the star. The wise men came to the house where the child was with his mother Mary. They bowed down and worshiped him. Then they opened the boxes of gifts they had brought for him. They gave him treasures of gold, frankincense, and myrrh. But God warned the wise men in a dream not to go back to Herod. So, they went home to their own country a different way. Matthew 2:9-12(ERV)

Prayer

Heavenly Father, let us enjoy the miracle of young children as they gaze upon the Christmas season with a twinkle in their eyes with the expectancy of all that Christmas brings. I remember some fond moments as a child myself. This Christmas let us reflect upon the wisemen who noticed the star, guiding them to Bethlam where little baby Jesus lay in a manger. Thank you for being our guide, our light for the path we follow Lord, in Jesus' name, Amen.

Day 27

Christmas is only one day of the year. It is a time when the light shines brightly during the darkest of times. Figuratively speaking, as is life. For some, Christmas can be unbearable because it reminds us how much light is absent from our lives.

We all endure our own struggles, disappointments, and at times, we are left feeling hopelessness. While our faith may falter from time to time, we must cling to hope.

During Jesus lifetime, he was raised under a corrupt dictatorship and challenging times for everyone. From zealotry to religious corruption. Jesus' birth was a time where light filtered through the darkness giving hope to all who listened and believed Him. God's timing is always perfect, blessing us with gifts of love, hope and charity.

Jesus taught his disciples to carry on as He did so we would carry forth His light on Christmas and every day of the year.

What struggles do you or have in the past struggled with?
What does the meaning of the "light of hope" mean to you?
How will you carry on the gifts of love, hope and charity in your life?

"You are the light that shines for the world to see. You are like a city built on a hill that cannot be hidden. People don't hide a lamp under a bowl. They put it on a lampstand. Then the light shines for everyone in the house. In the same way, you should be a light for other people. Live so that they will see the good things you do and praise your Father in heaven. Matthew 5:14-16 (ERV)

Prayer

Heavenly Father, thank you for coming into our lives and reminding us of this Christmas of your love for us through Jesus. As we have been blessed through your benevolence, show us how to be a light to others, bringing them love, hope, and charity. In Jesus' name, Amen.

Day 28

Blessings come in all different disguises during our lifetime. Sometimes as an unexpected gift, sometimes a prevention from making a huge mistake, and sometimes a prayer that is answered. I know if you're anything like me, the hope is that yours will be prayers answered instantly and all your dreams come to fruition. Wouldn't that be nice. However, God looks at the big picture and waits until the right time to keep you from making the wrong decision, and also to bless you with more than you asked for. So it is always best to practice gratitude and be happy with what you have, as a friend of mine hath said.

She went on to tell me how grateful she is to have been blessed with a loving family and how she has the best friends anyone can ask for. She feels her marriage to her husband is a blessing she once thought would never happen. But it did over twenty years ago. And to this day she loves how much of a gentleman he is, whether it is opening the car door for her or helping her around the home. My dear friend couldn't be more thankful and expressive about how God has showered her with blessings and she hasn't ever taken that for granted.

Have you ever taken for granted God's blessings?

How has God shown up in your life to keep you from making hasty decisions and later blessed you with something far greater?

Marriage should be honored by everyone. And every marriage should be kept pure between husband and wife.

I will never leave you; I will never run away from you. Hebrews 13:4-5 (ERV)

Prayer

Heavenly Father, thank you for your continued blessings and you from keeping me from making costly mistakes, especially with my relationships which I value so much. I pray this Christmas, you would soften the hearts of many, offering them another chance to discover what truly matters in this life, in Jesus' name, Amen.

Day 29

Many years ago, I used to paint commercial buildings. One client of mine was doing some extensive work at his dealership. I really enjoyed spending time with him, as we shared a lot of the same interests and values. I knew him so well that one day I came into the dealership and as we were discussing the plans, a few of his employees gathered and suggested making some other improvements first. After they all put their two cents in, he asked them if they had work to tend to and so they went back to their desks. As did he.

I went about my business and before leaving I went into his office and asked if something was wrong. Thinking about it for a moment he said, "Just once it would be nice if someone said, 'Thank you, nice job, the place is looking great, I am grateful for all the improvements you are making here.'"

I listened to him, and I believe it helped him to release his animosity. I nodded and agreed with him and said we all need to show a little bit more gratitude.

Sometimes people look at what is wrong, then praise people for the efforts they make when trying to help them and improve their surroundings.

This is so common in the workplace, but also at home, your neighbor's home, your sister's home, maybe yours also. Try this Christmas season to show some appreciation to everyone as you would like for yourself to be appreciated.

Have you ever done something for someone only to be less than gracious?

When you notice someone out of sorts, do you ever just listen?

How will you show appreciation to someone today, this Christmas season, and the following days after?

A cheerful heart is like good medicine, but a crushed spirit dries up the bones. Proverbs 17:22 (TLV)

Prayer

Heavenly Father, when someone does wrong by us or doesn't appreciate all we do, help us remember that is a reflection on them and not me. I know you see and hear everything and am forever grateful for everything you bestowed upon me. Help others see this, Lord. Help me not to be discouraged and to continue to do good in your eyes. This day and always let us show more appreciation for people's efforts and kindness, in Jesus' name, Amen.

Day 30

Christmas is a time of gathering, a time of reflection, a time of rest and a time to renew our minds. So, as we approach the New Year, take some time to thank God for His presence in your life and invite Him into every aspect this day forward.

Sometimes your plans may appear awkward, but rest assured they are not meant to harm you. The Lord will not allow your temptations to be greater than you can stand. And when we have endured, we will come out better and stronger than before. Therefore, we must be patient and trust God and His plans! What plans do you have? Are they in align with Gods?

For I know the plans I have for you," declares the Lord, "plans to prosper you and not to harm you, plans to give you hope and a future. Jeremiah 29:11

"I don't mean to say that I have already achieved these things or that I have already reached perfection. But I press on to possess that perfection for which Christ Jesus first possessed me. No, dear brothers and sisters, I have not achieved it, but I will focus on this one thing: Forgetting the past and looking forward to what lies ahead, I press on to reach the end of the race and receive the heavenly prize for which God, through Christ Jesus is calling us." Philippians 3:12-14

Life is a journey, not a destination as sometimes we perceive how we would like things to become. Living in the past is not where Jesus lives. He lives in the present and knows what the future holds.
What do you need to let go of from the past? How can you focus on what God has placed in your heart?

"But those who hope in the Lord will renew their strength. They will soar on wings like eagles; they will run and not grow weary; they will walk and not be faint." Isaiah 40:31

God is the creator of all things and people, whom we inherit our strength from, giving us hope to pursue dreams that we may otherwise give up upon. Have you any dreams that have not come to pass? Do not be dismayed. Give them to the Lord and He will give you strength to pursue all things in His name.

"And we know that God causes everything to work together for the good of those who love God and are called according to his purpose for them." Romans 8:28

Many times, life's challenges are God's way of bringing later dreams into reality, yet we don't see them now. We can be confident that the things we hope for will work in our favor.

What difficulties occurred in the past that later turned out to be a blessing?

Prayer

Heavenly Father, I am forever grateful for everything you have done and continue to show up and do for me in my life, even in times I may not even be aware of. I pray for you to transform me into a new person by changing the way I think as I take delight in you and your ways, in Jesus' name, Amen.

Bonus

Although Christmas is now past, Jesus proclaims a room for us in His Father's house as we fervently await His return. We experience all of God's goodness and glorious riches, that is why when we pray, we pray in Jesus' name.

Christmas is past but the joy of Christmas continues. The memories, our friends and families, our church family, and what God gave to us. Jesus.

The Holidays we know are a great way to enjoy social activities and being with people we love and sharing the presence of God Almighty. It's also a time to reflect upon the year past and even start a gratitude journal, if that's not something you already do. Make plans for the coming year and include God on your path. Start a bible reading either by yourself or with someone else. Maybe join one at your church.

Remember our time is precious and we are not promised tomorrow so jump on the band wagon and ride along.

Have you proclaimed your Faith?

What do you remember this past year God intervened and helped you?

Have you read the Bible? The story of Jesus?

I am the way, the truth, and the life. No one can come to the father except through me. John 14:6

Prayer

Heavenly Father, I look back and wonder what must have transpired when Jesus was born an infant and people traveled afar to see with their own eyes. How I marvel at the awesomeness of everything you do, please help me to always tell your story to others in a way that is pleasing to you, even when I am tired after all the worldly traditions of Christmas have ended, let your story continue, in Jesus' name, Amen.

My Motivation to Write Tidings of Comfort and Joy

Thank you for reading the preceding devotionals herein. I would also like to thank everyone who shared a little tidbit within the devotionals. I am grateful to my wife for her support and continued encouragement for me to follow my dreams and share with others what God has placed on my heart. And to my coach for her dedication and inspiration to keep writing and holding me accountable.

My hope is that you have grown spiritually and invited Jesus into every aspect of your life.

I have struggled the past few years with grief, health concerns, and some financial struggles I needed to address head-on. While at times it was very unpleasant, I know we all have times of uncertainties in life, so I know I'm not alone here and I didn't want anyone to feel Christmas was a time to "just get through"! Rather, it is a time to celebrate. A few of my friends shared some of their struggles with Christmas; and even more found Christmas a time to reflect upon memories, gratitude, and the opportunity to celebrate the birth of Jesus. The stories which were told to me were inspiring.

One morning, during a meeting with my coach, I reflected on the very first Christmas I shared with my wife Gina and how special it was. We moved into a new home together just before Christmas and were married in our living room on New Year's Eve. Since then, our Christmases together have been one blessing after another. For years we would have Christmas parties at our home up until the pandemic. We look forward to having those parties again to continue the traditions we began with a few friends and that we grew each year. Sometimes it was difficult to see everyone during the holidays, so the parties were especially fun.

Someone wrote to me stating although Christmas is only one day a year, a time of light in the darkest season.

You may not notice, but there are people around you who find Christmas unbearable because it reminds them how much light is missing from our lives. Feeling hopeless. Every Christmas, a tiny baby in a manger, with a glimpse of hope, brings light into the darkest valleys. Let us be that light for someone else.

A friend from high school shared some of her traditions from long ago. She had said, the anticipation of Christmas is as exciting as Christmas morning when she was a child. Every Thanksgiving, she and her mom prepare Thanksgiving dinner together until she passed away. At that time her dad stepped in, and they continued the tradition following football. On Christmas day, they celebrate Jesus' birth with cake and ice-cream. She is grateful for every day, living each day to the fullest, knowing tomorrow isn't promised, and she is grateful for God who gave these gifts to her family. She continues this tradition now with her son.

This is why we should never take anything or anyone for granted.

If you share some traditions with your family, I encourage you to invite someone less fortunate into your home for some Holiday cheer.

A little story about the cover of this book.

The creche was purchased from Bronner's, the largest Christmas store in the country. We used to spend countless days in Frankenmuth, Michigan, over the holidays, sometimes meeting our friends there. However, the nativity came from an antique store in Holly. We went there to watch a reenactment of the Dickens people in town. It was so cold and snowing with the wind whipping like many November evenings. So, we decided to go inside this little antique store around the corner. After searching for the last couple years, we finally found the nativity people we had been searching for as well. We had been to towns in Ohio and all over Michigan, but it was waiting for us in that antique store on a snowy afternoon in Holly, Michigan. The vintage figurines are made of porcelain, post-war era.

Let us not forget the "reason for the season".

May you all share the love of our Lord among each other and the "good news".

Love, prosperity, and good health to all. And to all God Bless you and be with you!

The Christmas Story

Taken and Combined from the Gospels of Matthew and Luke

Jesus' Birth Foretold

Now in the sixth month the angel Gabriel was sent from God to a city in Galilee named Nazareth, to a virgin betrothed to a man whose name was Joseph, of the descendants of David; and the virgin's name was Mary. And coming in, he said to her, "Greetings, favored one! The Lord *is* with you." But she was very perplexed at *this* statement, and was pondering what kind of greeting this was. And the angel said to her, "Do not be afraid, Mary, for you have found favor with God. And behold, you will conceive in your womb and give birth to a son, and you shall name Him Jesus. He will be great and will be called the Son of the Most High; and the Lord God will give Him the throne of His father David; and He will reign over the house of Jacob forever, and His kingdom will have no end."

But Mary said to the angel, "How will this be, since I am a virgin?"

The angel answered and said to her, "The Holy Spirit will come upon you, and the power of the Most High will overshadow you; for that reason also the holy Child will be called the Son of God. And behold, even your relative Elizabeth herself has conceived a son in her old age, and she who was called infertile is now in her sixth month. For nothing will be impossible with God."

And Mary said, "Behold, the Lord's bond-servant; may it be done to me according to your word." And the angel departed from her. Luke 1:26-38 (NASB)

Now the birth of Jesus the Messiah was as follows: when His mother Mary had been betrothed to Joseph, before they came together she was found to be pregnant by the Holy Spirit. And her husband Joseph, since he was a righteous man and did not want to disgrace her, planned to send her away secretly. But when he had thought this over, behold, an angel of the Lord appeared to him in a dream, saying, "Joseph, son of David, do not be afraid to take Mary as your wife; for the Child who has been conceived in her is of the Holy Spirit. She will give birth to a Son; and you shall name Him Jesus, for He will save His people from their sins." Now all this took place so that what was spoken by the Lord through the prophet would be fulfilled: "Behold, the virgin will conceive and give birth to a son, and they shall call him Immanuel " which translated means, God with us. Joseph awoke from his sleep and did as the angel of the Lord commanded him, and took *Mary* as his wife, but kept her a virgin until she gave birth to a Son; and he named Him Jesus. Matthew 1: 18-25 (NASB)

Jesus' birth in Bethlehem

This was the first census taken while Quirinius was governor of Syria. And all *the people* were on their way to register for the census, each to his own city. Now Joseph also went up from Galilee, from the city of Nazareth, to Judea, to the city of David which is called Bethlehem, because he was of the house and family of David, in order to register along with Mary, who was betrothed to him, and was pregnant. While they were there, the time came for her to give birth. And she gave birth to her firstborn son; and she wrapped Him in cloths, and laid Him in a manger, because there was no room for them in the inn. Luke 2:1-7 (NASB)

The visit of Magi

Now after Jesus was born in Bethlehem of Judea in the days of Herod the king, behold, magi from the east arrived in Jerusalem, saying, "Where is He who has been born King of the Jews? For we saw His star in the east and have come to worship Him." When Herod the king heard *this*, he was troubled, and all Jerusalem with him. And gathering together all the chief priests and scribes of the people, he inquired of them where the Messiah was to be born. They said to him, "In Bethlehem of Judea; for this is what has been written by the prophet. "And you, Bethlehem, land of Judah, are by no means least among the leaders of Judah; for from you will come forth a ruler who will shepherd my people of Israel."
Then Herod secretly called for the magi and determined from them the exact time the star appeared. And he sent them to Bethlehem and said, "Go and search carefully for the Child; and when you have found *Him*, report to me, so that I too may come and worship Him." After hearing the king, they went on their way; and behold, the star, which they had seen in the east, went on ahead of them until it came to a stop

over *the place* where the Child was *to be found*. When they saw the star, they rejoiced exceedingly with great joy. And after they came into the house, they saw the Child with His mother Mary; and they fell down and worshiped Him. Then they opened their treasures and presented to Him gifts of gold, frankincense, and myrrh. And after being warned *by God* in a dream not to return to Herod, *the magi* left for their own country by another way. Matthew 2: 1-12 (BASB)

The Shepherds visited by the Angles

In the same region there were *some* shepherds staying out in the fields and keeping watch over their flock at night. And an angel of the Lord *suddenly* stood near them, and the glory of the Lord shone around them; and they were terribly frightened. And *so* the angel said to them, "Do not be afraid; for behold, I bring you good news of great joy which will be for all the people; for today in the city of David there has been born for you a Savior, who is Christ the Lord. And this *will be* a sign for you: you will find a baby wrapped in clothes and lying in a]manger." And suddenly there appeared with the angel a multitude of the heavenly army *of angels* praising God and saying, "Glory to God in the highest, and on earth peace among people with whom He is pleased."
When the angels had departed from them into heaven, the shepherds *began* saying to one another, "Let's go straight to Bethlehem, then, and see this thing that has happened, which the Lord has made known to us." And they came in a hurry and found their way to Mary and Joseph, and the baby as He lay in the manger. When they had seen *Him*, they made known the statement which had been told about this Child. And all who heard it were amazed about the things which were told to them by the shepherds. But Mary treasured all these things, pondering them in her heart. And the shepherds went back, glorifying and praising God for all that they had heard and seen, just as had been told them.
Luke 2:8-20 (NASB)

Guests

Who visited and who did you visit?

Gifts and Giving

My Christmas wish list! Gift list for others!

Christmas Memories

What do I want to remember?

Acts of Kindness

Who did I make a better Christmas for? Did you volunteer somewhere? Invite a neighbor to share Christmas dinner?

_____

_____

_____

_____

_____

_____

_____

_____

_____

_____

_____

_____

_____

_____

_____

_____

_____

_____

_____

Additional Resources

Follow me for updates concerning upcoming devotionals and other resources:

Follow me on Facebook:
https://www.facebook.com/3Pslivinnow

Follow me on Instagram:
https://www.instagram.com/thomas_bratton_author/

Follow me on LinkedIn:
https://www.linkedin.com/in/thomas-bratton-baab9244/

Follow me on Pinterest:
https://www.pinterest.com/becominganchoredtb/

Follow me on Goodreads:
https://www.goodreads.com/author/show/22971770.Thomas_Bratton

Visit my website and encouraging blog:
https://thomasbrattonauthor.com/

Becoming Anchored

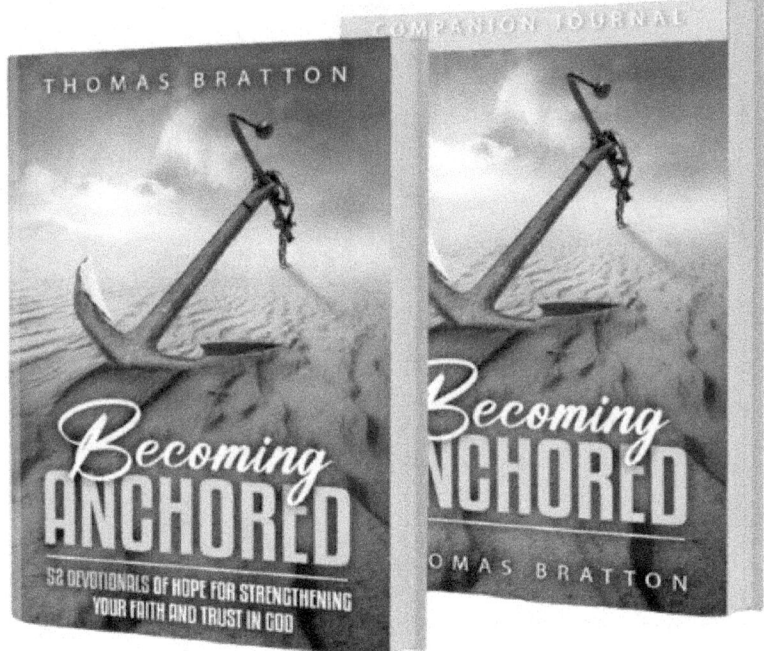

Start your year by becoming anchored in Christ to strengthen your faith and hope.

Thank You

Thank you again for reading. If this devotional has blessed you, would you be so kind as to leave your honest review for me on the book page? It really helps authors promote their work, reach more readers, and impact more lives. Then, would you share it with a friend? Thank you.

www.ingramcontent.com/pod-product-compliance
Lightning Source LLC
Chambersburg PA
CBHW070342010526
44107CB00004B/599